Truths

Truths

Nigel Fulmore-Smith

Charleston, SC
www.PalmettoPublishing.com

Truths

First Edition

Paperback ISBN: 979-8-88590-859-7

Contents

Apparent Truths Pt. 1

The apparent truth is
I will die one day.
My sins will be paid.

I will walk in Heaven
hopefully,
Like an innocent deer.

One day I will learn to face
My prevalent fears.
I will die one day.

And when that day comes-
I will be ready.
Another apparent truth

is that I love,
and when I love,
I love hard.

I probably love too densely.
Maybe I take things too far.
But when I love,

I like to show how it's true.
I will love from the outside
to the person's deepest roots.

I will love wholly,
and one day
I will acquire the love that I've been giving.

Lukewarm Coffee

I don't want to be lukewarm.
I want to burn with a fire that
can scold the devil's tongue.
I want to burn brighter than the hottest sun.

I want to burn longer than the burning bush.
I want to burn hot.

Hotter than Monday morning
coffee. You know the kind.

The kind I pour to get me through the day.
The kind I pour that helps me deal with
Lisa and Joe, or Jamez and LeToya.
I want to burn like that coffee.

I want to burn for you
Lord.

But naturally, I'm more like other coffee.
Coffee that when poured was hot but has
now sat out for too long. Doing nothing.

Coffee that has lost its steam.
Coffee that when you sip, does
not taste the same.

It lost flavor with its heat.

I don't want to be lukewarm.

But do I love you, Lord?

Do I love you
like a son would love his mother?
Running into her arms every
time he wounds himself.

Or, do I love this world
like a dog would love his vomit?
Engulfing its contents like he
forgot it does not taste good.

Maybe I should stick to being cold. At least
the biggest trend in America is iced coffee.
At least that's what I'm used to. At least
I do that well.

I could learn to be hot.
I should burn hotter than Anglo-
Saxons on Florida beaches.
I should burn brighter than the sun,

but even the hottest suns burn
out at some point.
And even the hottest coffee starts to get cold.

I don't want to be lukewarm.
Lukewarm coffee never tastes good.

And It always gets spewed out of your mouth.

Tonight

Tonight is the night that he
can finally speak up.
He finally has the courage to say how he feels.
His heart will not hold back.
It won't be concealed.

Tonight, two hearts will finally meet.
And share true love forever.
These two cannot be severed.

Tonight, he gets the one for his soul.
And in the morn, his face will have a smile.
He knows she'll be there for a while.

Her

Laying in the starry night.
Looking into her starry eyes.
Finally feeling the destined bliss,
Followed by her soft kiss.

Unwritten Vows

As I glance at the person from my dreams,
I've realized that beautiful gleam,
Doesn't come from me,
But our creation.

I love you.

I love the way you smile.
I love the way you love our child.
I love your insecurities, pure.
You've loved mine when I didn't have the cure.

I didn't have the cure for my own faults.

And yet, you still have taken me in.
To your heart and mind.
And with time being around.
We have united to make this marriage sound.

She Loved a Man

She loved a man that never loved her back
because he gave her things that
she could never grasp;
desires that existed under her mask.

She loved a man, whose heart
was made of stone.
He never knew of a thing called a happy home.
He felt destined to always be alone

She loved a man that never understood love.
Never able to sacrifice for the
ones he puts above.
He didn't believe in the power of a shove.

She loved a man who never saw his wealth.
Value to him was his
accomplishments and health.
For she loved a man who never loved himself.

A Woman's Heart Taken

Instead of trying to open her legs
Why don't you open her mind?
Try to give her love,
Instead of wasting her time.

Make sure she's okay
When she isn't acting the same.
Think of what you can do for her,
Instead of thinking of what you can gain.

A Man's Heart Taken

You should support his dreams
Instead of holding him at fault.
Love his insecurities
Despite what they cause.

Protect his heart
From others that plot to destroy.
And don't be a stressor
But the cause of his joy.

Ode to Myself (I Love You)

I love you.

I love the way you laugh,
and I love the way you smile.

I love how you jog a yard,
instead of running a mile.

I love when you see someone in distress,
and ask if they need you.

I love when you're hurt
and remain strong when someone leaves you.

I love how you love others,
and always aim to give.

I love when you're depressed.
and still, proclaim to live.

I love how you're free
and share that freedom with others.

I love how you view women and men,
and treat them as sisters and brothers.

After all these years of being mistreated
and feeling so defeated…

After all this time
of leaving self-love behind…

      I finally
            love you.

Chauvin

I don't feel no ways tired. Come too
far from where I've started from.

Derek Chauvin,
a boogeyman for all black boys and girls.

An officer who took a knee
like Kapernick, he too had a protest

But his protest was our
complexion, our magic,
Jesus in our flesh.

His protest was to kill what was inside,
but can I let you in on a little secret?

Mr. Chauvin,
you cannot kill what God has created.

When one voice dies,
another one multiplies.

Our magic is a honeycomb
and our blackness is pollinating
the world like bees;

Bearing flowers and oxygen
for future children to breathe.

Mr. Chauvin, what were you thinking?
Did you believe that you could kill hope?

When even slavery produced music and fruit
 and a search for the Savior.

Mr. Chauvin, you did not kill hope,
you produced it.

You reminded me that my hope is
not in this tent we call the world.
My hope is in the loving arms of my Savior

The one whose blood is our hope
The one whose hands and feet were pierced
for our transgression, did not lose hope.
The one who kept on singing
as he went onto Calvary

Did
Not
Lose
Hope.

I imagine Jesus singing this song
before it ever came to be.
Humming it as he carried his cross.

Singing it on the road he was
traveling on and believing
that His Father would never leave him.

*Nobody told me that the road would
be easy, and I don't believe He's
brought me this far to leave me.*

Held

Newborn babies are so small, and
fragile that you must be careful
when holding their tiny heads.

You must be careful, lest you hold
them too hard, and hurt them
Damage them before they
are able to truly live.

I wonder if God looks at us in this way.
Making sure that he is careful to hold us.
To remind us we are safe, close to his
bosom, and loved in an infinite way.

Sticks and Stones

They say sticks and stones may break your
bones but words will never hurt you.
Well, I beg to differ.

When my coworker told me that
I acted like a white boy

Those words shattered my bones,
Ground them into the powder she
would use for her makeup

She left me paralyzed from the waist down.

My blackness was truly dissected
and picked apart for her pleasure.

I had to dive into Jesus because he's
the only one that could resurrect it.

I felt ashamed to say I was
black for one second.
I admit it.

I had to see if there was enough slang in
my throat to consider myself black.

Did I need to sag my pants, smoke
some weed, or go to jail?
Karen is that all blackness is to you?

And yes I called you Karen because your
real name is not worth exclaiming.

So, Karen

did you know prophets ain't
welcome in their own homes
and black folk ain't welcome in the
country they were brought to?

Did you know that

blackness is not a row of dead
bodies in the street,
killed by their infatuation with
drugs, money, and fame?

blackness is not a uniform personality,

where everyone acts the same.

We have a deviation of character.
So, please teach me,

Rabbi of black culture
because apparently I've been fooled.
I've been bamboozled by busy black brothers

and matriarchal mothers.

I've been fooled by cookouts, family
gatherings, and weddings too.

I do not have all the answers,
and neither, do you.

Karen did you know
To be black

in America
is to be told you must behave a certain way,

and if you do no,

the colonizers
will throw sticks and stones to hurt you.

David

Sometimes I feel like David. I feel faithful.
Like when he fought Goliath, swinging
his slingshot, and focusing on God
instead of the Giant in front of him.

Sometimes I feel like David. I feel hopeless.
Like every psalm I sing is a call to bring
the hope of the Lord back into my heart.

Sometimes I feel like David. I feel stuck
watching my lust kill every lovely thing in
my heart. Falling deeper into temptation,
doing everything I can to have her. To
be alone with her, instead of God.

Walking on Water

I wonder how Peter felt to walk on water.
To feel unsettling waves beneath his feet.
To look in the loving eyes of Jesus.
To feel the strength of the wind on his cheeks.

I wonder how Peter felt when
he fell into the water.
The shame of his eyes gone
astray sank him further.

The sound of the winds cackling laughter.
The waves compress his chest as he
sees the hand of his beloved Savior,

Reaching out

In the depth of the waters

With no shame or judgment on His face.

I wonder how Peter felt
To doubt God
and
        be
                rescued
                        by
                                Him
                                        in
                                                the same breath.

Till

I want to love you till I return to dust;
till my flesh no longer cries out
cause you are not in my rib.

I want to love you till Jesus comes back;
till we're mad cause our forever
honeymoon was interrupted.

I want to love you till we go to Heaven;
till we become angels in God's choir

and we make subtle glances
and remember the times we
worshipped till we cried.

I want to love you till the stars get jealous.
till they scream because you are the
only star that lights my life.

I want to love you till I get tired of loving you.
and I don't think I will ever get tired.

Angels

When angels visit earth, why
must they return?
Why would God allow such beauty
to only be here for a moment;
To only exist in a plane that has
destruction, violence, and greed.

I do not know why you would come here,
Only to reside for a moment.
But when you return,

Can you ask God
If I may I visit you
Every once in a while?